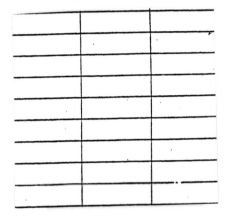

WE THE PEOPLE

Williamsburg

by Judy Alter

Content Adviser: Dr. Julie Richter, Consultant, Colonial Williamsburg Foundation

Reading Adviser: Dr. Linda D. Labbo,
Department of Reading Education, College of Education,
The University of Georgia

COMPASS POINT BOOKS
Minneapolis, Minnesota

Compass Point Books
3722 West 50th Street, #115
Minneapolis, MN 55410

Visit Compass Point Books on the Internet at *www.compasspointbooks.com* or e-mail your request
to *custserv@compasspointbooks.com*

Editors: E. Russell Primm, Emily J. Dolbear, Sarah E. De Capua, and Catherine Neitge
Photo Researcher: Svetlana Zhurkina
Photo Selector: Linda S. Koutris
Designer/Page Production: Bradfordesign Inc./The Design Lab
Cartographer: XNR Productions, Inc.

Library of Congress Cataloging-in-Publication Data

Alter, Judy, 1938–
  Williamsburg / by Judy Alter.
     v. cm. — (We the people)
 Includes bibliographical references and index.
 Contents: The beginnings—The Virginia Colony—The founding of Williamsburg—The General
Assembly—Restoration—Visiting historic Williamsburg.
  ISBN 0-7565-0300-0
  1. Williamsburg (Va.)—History—Juvenile literature. [1. Williamsburg (Va.)—History.] I. Title.
II. We the people (Compass Point Books)
  F234.W7 .A57 2002
  975.5'4252—dc21   2002002959

TABLE OF CONTENTS

The Beginnings 4

The Virginia Colony 6

The Founding of Williamsburg 9

The General Assembly 24

Restoring Williamsburg 31

Visiting Colonial Williamsburg 35

Glossary 42

Did You Know? 43

Important Dates 44

Important People 45

Want to Know More? 46

Index 48

THE BEGINNINGS

Williamsburg was the capital of the **colony** of Virginia from 1699 until 1780. The Virginia **House of Burgesses** was located in Williamsburg as well. Several of the men who later founded the United States served in the Virginia House of Burgesses. The founders helped to form the ideas that are the basis for American **democracy.** This made Williamsburg an important city in the history of the United States.

The House of Burgesses held meetings at the old capitol in Williamsburg, Virginia.

Today, the city's historic area is the world's largest living-history museum. Each year, more than 1 million visitors from all over the world come to Virginia to tour Williamsburg. Five hundred restored or reconstructed buildings and 90 acres (36 hectares) of beautiful gardens occupy 173 acres (70 ha). Williamsburg is an outstanding example of the preservation of American history.

The Governor's Palace is one of many historic sites in Williamsburg.

5

THE VIRGINIA COLONY

The first settlers from England landed at Jamestown, Virginia, on the James River in 1607. Jamestown was the first permanent English colony in North America. It was the capital of the colony of Virginia before Williamsburg.

Life was hard for these English settlers before they learned to grow tobacco. They grew the plant on large

The first meeting of the House of Burgesses took place in Jamestown in 1619.

and small plantations throughout the colony. Tobacco became the most important crop in the colony and was exported to England.

In the 1700s, Virginia was the largest British colony in size and in population. It had many plantations, or large farms, that usually grew only one crop. Plantations were like small towns. Most plantations had a kitchen, a dairy, a laundry, a smokehouse, a coach house, and a stable. The plantation owner's family lived in a mansion. Supervisors called overseers and **tenant farmers** might have small houses on the property.

A successful plantation owner had eight to ten slaves. These slaves worked in the fields growing tobacco. Sometimes the plantation owner also had workers called **indentured servants.**

The plantation owner's children learned from their elders and from books about history and politics. A planter might also hire a tutor to teach his sons and daughters.

A plantation owner and his wife are greeted by their slaves.

Some boys attended the nearby College of William and Mary. Others traveled to England to study at schools there. They learned to run the plantation. These young men were also trained to help govern the colony. They became members of the House of Burgesses. They also helped to establish the democracy that governs the United States today.

THE FOUNDING OF WILLIAMSBURG

Eventually, there were many problems with Jamestown as the colony's capital. The statehouse had burned down four times. Also, the town had been built on a swamp. As a result, it was damp and full of disease-carrying mosquitoes.

In 1633, a settlement was established inland from Jamestown. It was called Middle Plantation. In 1699, the colonial government moved from Jamestown to Middle Plantation. The College of William and Mary and Bruton Parish Church were both located there. Middle Plantation was also a healthier location than Jamestown. The city was renamed Williamsburg in honor of King William III of England.

Williamsburg was laid out according to a plan provided by Governor Francis Nicholson. He represented the British government in Virginia. Governor Nicholson's plan included public buildings, streets, and the public square. It also included a street 99 feet (30 meters) wide running from one end of the city to the other. It was called Duke of Gloucester Street.

The College of William and Mary stood at the western end of this street. Founded in 1693, it is the second-oldest institution of higher learning in America. (Harvard is the oldest.) Four American presidents—George Washington, Thomas Jefferson, James Monroe, and John Tyler—studied at William and Mary.

The College of William and Mary in Williamsburg, Virginia

Duke of Gloucester Street as it looks today

The capitol was built at the eastern end of the
street between 1701 and 1705. The colonists were afraid
it might burn like the capitol at Jamestown. At first, the
new capitol had no fireplaces and neither candles nor

pipes were allowed. Fireplaces were eventually added. The capitol did burn in January 1747, but it was rebuilt by 1753. The capitol was the scene of dances, suppers, and social events, as well as legislative meetings.

The home of Virginia's governor stood at the end of Palace Street and faced Palace Green. Construction lasted from 1706 until 1722. When completed, the residence was one of the grandest public buildings in the thirteen colonies. People called it the Palace.

The Governor's Palace had offices in separate buildings, elaborate gardens with walkways, a canal, a stable, a carriage house, a kitchen, a laundry, an eight-sided bathhouse, and an unusual **cupola.** The building was the center of the city's social life and entertainment. Every year, the birthday of the king of England was celebrated with a large party.

The Palace burned in 1781 and in 1782, Virginia's leaders decided to sell the bricks from the burned buildings. The remaining buildings were in ruins by 1835. In

Both parties and government meetings took place in Williamsburg's capitol.

13

1862, during the Civil War (1861–1865), Union soldiers occupying Williamsburg used bricks from the ruins to build chimneys in their huts.

Bruton Parish Church faced Duke of Gloucester Street. Like the Governor's Palace, it was set back on a grassy plot. After it was founded in 1674, the first Bruton Parish Church was completed in 1683. The present

The Governor's Palace

structure—the third church at this location—was built between 1712 and 1715. It was enlarged in 1752, and an English organ was installed in the church in 1755. The church was so important in the life of the colony that it had its own representative in the Virginia General Assembly. Bruton Parish Church still has many members today.

The powder magazine stood in the center of Market Square. This eight-sided brick

Bruton Parish Church got its steeple in 1769.

15

The powder magazine, where the colonists stored guns and ammunition, was built in 1715.

structure stored the colony's arms and ammunition. On the night of April 20, 1775, the British governor, John Murray Dunmore, ordered British marines to take gunpowder from this structure. The Gunpowder Incident helped convince Virginians that they should declare their independence from England. After the American Revolution (1775–1783), residents of Williamsburg used the powder magazine as a market, a Baptist meetinghouse, a dancing school, and a stable. In 1889, the Association for the Preservation of Virginia **Antiquities** bought the building, repaired it, and opened it as a museum.

Governor Nicholson's plan also included what the houses in Williamsburg should look like. Each was built on ½ acre (0.2 ha) of land. This allowed plenty of space for gardens and small orchards. Houses were to be set a

Duke of Gloucester Street in the late nineteenth century

17

This room of the Governor's Palace is decorated with wallpaper and wainscoting.

certain distance back from the street. The typical house was 1½ stories high with a steep shingled roof and a chimney at one or both ends of the house. The houses were wooden because it cost more to build a brick house. The windows were evenly spaced in a simple pattern.

Inside, many of the houses had white plaster walls. Some homeowners painted the walls blue or green. Others put up flowered or patterned wallpaper. The wallpaper often had a Chinese design, which was popular in England at the time. Sometimes there was chair-high wainscoting. In wainscoting, the lower portion of a wall is finished differently from the upper portion. It was seen more often in public buildings, such as the capitol and the Palace. Some houses simply had a chair rail attached to the walls to keep chairs from damaging the paint or wallpaper. Many Williamsburg residents hung engravings or mirrors on the walls.

Furniture was either imported from England or constructed to look like English furniture. Most of it was

This bedroom in the Governor's Palace has a four-poster bed with a canopy.

mahogany. Some Williamsburg craftsmen made furniture out of pine. Most floors were bare wood with an occasional small carpet or painted floor cloth. A spinet or harpsichord, keyboard instruments similar to a piano, might be seen in the living room. In the bedrooms, the town's wealthy residents often had four-poster beds with canopies. Sometimes a trundle bed slid out from under the larger

20

bed. A trundle bed is a low bed on wheels for guests.

A fireplace in almost every room provided heat. Candles supplied light. Today, such houses would seem very cold and dark.

The kitchen was a separate building to avoid the danger of fire. It also kept heat and cooking odors out of the main house. Most houses also had a dairy and a smokehouse. Meat or fish was preserved with dense smoke in the smokehouse. Stables or coach houses were also on many properties.

Properties often had smaller buildings such as a kitchen or woodshed a short distance from the main house.

Many Williamsburg houses had formal gardens. Hedges were carefully trimmed into squares, triangles, wedges, and ovals. Brick walkways in the gardens were laid out in patterns. Sometimes these walkways were constructed of crushed shells, washed pebbles, or even soil. In one garden, the shaped hedges and connecting walkways looked like a simple British flag! The gardens had seats for people to enjoy the scenery, but they did not

The formal gardens at the Governor's Palace

have decorative statues or garden houses. Most of the gardens had fallen into ruin before the twentieth-century **restoration** of the city.

By order of King George I of England, Williamsburg became a city in 1722. Williamsburg was never as large as Boston, New York City, or Philadelphia. It had slightly more than 200 houses, and its population was never more than 2,000 people. Many people made their living as craftsmen. They worked as cabinetmakers and silversmiths. Others worked as tavern keepers. The city was never a major manufacturing center.

A silversmith working in Williamsburg today

THE GENERAL ASSEMBLY

The Virginia General Assembly was modeled after the British government. It consisted of two houses. The lower house, called the House of Burgesses, was like Britain's House of Commons. The upper house, or the Council of State, resembled Britain's House of Lords. Most of its members were wealthy plantation owners or the sons of wealthy plantation owners.

The General Assembly met twice a

Members of the House of Burgesses discuss the business of the colonies.

24

year in Williamsburg. The meetings were usually held in the spring and the fall. People from all over the colony came to Williamsburg for publick times when the General Assembly was in session. Publick times were like country fairs. The people enjoyed elegant dinners, dances, horse races, and

Horse races are a part of today's publick times celebrations at Colonial Williamsburg.

25

performances by traveling theater troupes. Stores displayed the latest fashions from Britain, including wigs made of human hair.

Until the 1760s, Virginia colonists were loyal to the British Crown. But after 1763, England began to pass laws that angered the colonists.

In 1763, King George III signed a proclamation that prohibited the colonists from settling on land west of the Appalachian Mountains. This upset colonists who wanted to move into that territory.

On April 5, 1764, the king imposed the Revenue Act (also known as the Sugar Act). This act forced colonists to pay taxes on sugar. The taxes would help pay for running the colony's government.

The Quartering Act of May 1765 ordered colonists to allow British troops to live in their homes. They also had to provide troops with food and supplies.

The Currency Act, signed by the king on April 19, 1764, declared that the colonies could not issue paper

The Quartering Act said British soldiers could force colonists to give them food and lodging. **27**

money. Virginia had issued a large amount of paper money to finance the French and Indian War (1754–1763). In that war, Britain fought France for control of parts of North America. The colonists continued to use the colony's paper money after Britain's victory, which angered the king.

But the Stamp Act of March 1765 was the greatest blow.

British tax stamps were placed on newspapers, pamphlets, playing cards, and legal papers.

It required colonists to place stamps on newspapers, pamphlets, playing cards, and legal papers. These stamps, which were similar to taxes, had to be purchased from the British government.

The Stamp Act upset Virginians and residents of the other twelve colonies. They began to meet and discuss British laws because they believed these laws violated their freedom as Americans. By 1776, many of the colonists and their leaders wanted to declare their independence from England.

On May 15, 1776, the Virginia Convention instructed its delegates to the Continental Congress in Philadelphia to propose independence from Great Britain. Virginia was the first colony to make this proposal.

In 1780, at the height of the American Revolution, the capital of Virginia was moved from Williamsburg to Richmond. The state's leaders thought Richmond would be a safer seat of government during the war. It was also more centrally located in Virginia. Today, Richmond continues to serve as Virginia's state capital.

Williamsburg's population declined when the capital was moved to Richmond, but the city remained important. It had a college, the first psychiatric institution in the nation, and a regional market. During the Civil War, many of Williamsburg's historic buildings were destroyed.

The Virginia state capitol in Richmond

RESTORING WILLIAMSBURG

In 1926, Dr. W. A. R. Goodwin, minister of Bruton Parish Church, made an ambitious proposal. He wanted to buy the original city of Williamsburg, including historic houses. He also suggested founding an organization to do this work. The organization became the Colonial Williams-burg Foundation. Its purpose was to recover America's colonial period—the time before America became an independent nation. By restoring the buildings, Goodwin hoped that the lifestyle of the times could also be reclaimed.

John D. Rockefeller Jr.

Goodwin enlisted the support of millionaire **philan-thropist** John D. Rockefeller Jr. to pay for the project. Rockefeller donated generously throughout the restoration.

The restoration staff included architects, archaeologists, gardeners, builders, town planners, historians, lawyers, engineers, and hundreds of volunteers. The staff did thorough research about life in colonial Williamsburg. Old maps and drawings by Thomas Jefferson contributed greatly to the project. Researchers also used pictures of the capitol, the Palace, and the College of William and Mary found in the library at Oxford University in England. The possessions of Lord Botetourt, who served as governor from 1768 to 1776, provided detailed information about the Palace furnishings.

After the houses were cleaned out, the restoration staff took measurements, drew sketches, and collected color samples from layers of original paint. They also carefully studied walks, brickwork, floors, partitions, decorations, stairs, mantels, doors, and windows.

Historians figured out what grew in the gardens and what animals were kept. Gardeners removed overgrown plants and trees. In one instance, forsythia, a shrub with yellow flowers, had been planted in many gardens. After they discovered that forsythia was not introduced to America until the 1800s, gardeners removed all of the forsythia shrubs from the grounds!

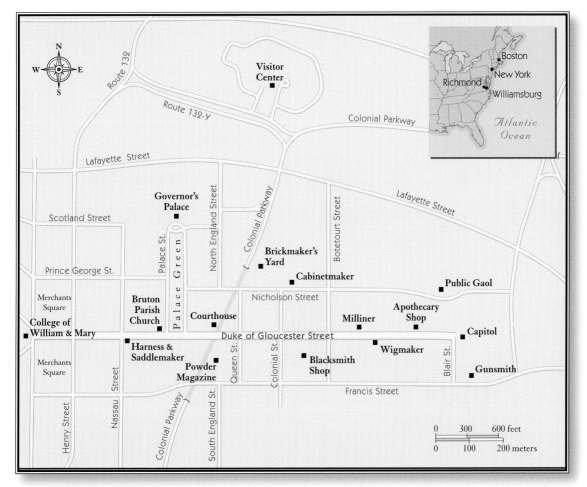

A map of Williamsburg

This building is a reconstruction of Williamsburg's capitol.

When possible, buildings were restored rather than rebuilt. Walls and floors were given new supports. The capitol and the Governor's Palace had to be completely rebuilt. Builders put both structures on their original foundations and used old materials as much as they could. Some houses were rebuilt on old foundations, too. Authentic furnishings or reproductions of objects from the 1700s decorated major buildings and small houses.

VISITING COLONIAL WILLIAMSBURG

Today, Colonial Williamsburg is a living, working city. Some employees of the Colonial Williamsburg Foundation live with their families in historic buildings not open to the public. Many other buildings are open for tours. Some restored homes take in overnight guests.

A private home in historic Williamsburg

35

It takes more than one day to see all of Colonial Williamsburg. At the Visitor Center, people can decide what they want to see and watch a video of the city's history. Since no cars are allowed in Colonial Williamsburg, many people take carriage or wagon rides.

Visitors to Williamsburg's restored historic area see what life was like for the colonists.

Visitors do more than just see the historic area. They become involved in the life of the city as it was in the 1700s. Workers called interpreters wear colonial-era costumes and lead visitors through many activities. Tradesmen make shoes, furniture, wigs, buckets, and other products from colonial times. They are glad to discuss their work and to explain its details. They greet visitors to the taverns, stoke the fires outside houses, and re-create life as it was on the eve of the American Revolution.

Working as shoemakers, these interpreters help bring Colonial Williamsburg to life for visitors.

37

At Colonial Williamsburg, revolutionaries and loyalists to the British Crown argue vigorously in taverns. Visitors may hear interpreters dressed as George Washington, Thomas Jefferson, and Patrick Henry make a case against British taxes and discuss the idea of a free America. Public officials, soldiers, loyalists, patriots, slaves, and housewives all have opinions. Careful to remain in character, each town resident speaks eagerly to visitors.

Interpreters at the courthouse reenact typical trials of the 1700s. Visitors sit on the jury. They can set a man free, or send him to the stocks. They can put their own arms and legs into the wooden stocks to see what it felt like to be an eighteenth-century offender.

At Colonial Williamsburg, people exchange modern-day money for colonial-era money. Many people take colonial money home as a souvenir. Others use the money during their visit. Shops in the historic area sell three-cornered hats, decorative bonnets, quills and ink,

At Colonial Williamsburg, interpreters discuss issues of the nation.

block-printed stationery and sealing wax, candles, soaps, jams, hams, brass, pewter, and jewelry. The money spent at Colonial Williamsburg helps maintain the historic area.

Some young people rent colonial-style costumes for the day. Today's visitors have a hard time imagining life without running water, computers, television, and telephones. Williamsburg gives them an idea of what life was like in America when it was still a British colony.

This shop in Colonial Williamsburg sells many items from colonial times.

41

GLOSSARY

antiquities—objects used in an earlier time

colony—a territory settled by people from another country and controlled by that country

cupola—a small structure on top of a roof that sometimes holds a light or a bell

democracy—a form of government in which the people elect their leaders

House of Burgesses—the representative assembly of colonial Virginia

indentured servants—people who work for someone else for a certain period of time in return for payment of travel and living costs

philanthropist—a person who gives time or money to help others

restoration—the act of bringing something back to its former condition

tenant farmers—workers who farm on land that they rent for cash or for a share of the crops or livestock

DID YOU KNOW?

- Williamsburg is the home of the first public psychiatric hospital in America. It was founded in 1773 and is still in operation today. It is called Eastern State Hospital.

- Virginia's first governor, Patrick Henry, is best remembered for the words "Give me liberty or give me death." His fiery speeches inspired the demand for freedom that led to the American Revolution.

- Colonial Williamsburg has a staff of 3,500 workers and about 800 volunteers.

- You can send a postcard from Colonial Williamsburg—with a postmark from the eighteenth century!

- At Colonial Williamsburg, you can buy traditional animal crackers in the shape of animals from colonial times. They include Leicester longwool sheep, American cream draft horses, American milking red Devon cows, Canadian horses, and Hamburg roosters and hens.

IMPORTANT DATES

Timeline

1607	First English settlers land at Jamestown, Virginia.
1633	Middle Plantation settlement is established inland from Jamestown.
1699	Virginia's capital moves to Middle Plantation and is now called Williamsburg.
1722	The Governor's Palace is completed; King George I declares Williamsburg a city.
1775	The American Revolution begins.
1780	Virginia's capital moves to Richmond.
1783	The American Revolution ends.
1889	The Association for the Preservation of Virginia Antiquities buys the Williamsburg powder magazine as a museum.
1926	Dr. W. A. R. Goodwin starts work on Williamsburg's historic area with funds from John D. Rockefeller Jr.
1932	The first building in Colonial Williamsburg opens to the public.

IMPORTANT PEOPLE

W. A. R. GOODWIN

(1869–1939), *the minister of Bruton Parish Church who began the restoration project in Williamsburg*

PATRICK HENRY

(1736–1799), *a lawyer, an advocate of liberty, a member of the Virginia House of Burgesses, and the first governor of the state of Virginia*

THOMAS JEFFERSON

(1743–1826), *a Virginia plantation owner, a member of the Virginia House of Burgesses, a Continental Congress delegate, an author of the Declaration of Independence, and the third president of the United States from 1801 to 1809*

JOHN D. ROCKEFELLER JR.

(1839–1937), *the only son of businessman John D. Rockefeller and a philanthropist whose Rockefeller Foundation funded many projects, including the Williamsburg restoration project*

WANT TO KNOW MORE?

At the Library

Anderson, Joan Wilkins. *A Williamsburg Household.* Boston: Houghton Mifflin, 1990.

Brenner, Barbara, and Jennie Williams. *If You Lived in Williamsburg in Colonial Days.* New York: Scholastic, 2000.

Kent, Zachary. *Williamsburg.* Chicago: Childrens Press, 1992.

Nixon, Joan Lowery. *Caesar's Story: 1759.* New York: Bantam Doubleday Dell Books for Young Readers, 2000.

Nixon, Joan Lowery. *Maria's Story: 1773.* New York: Random House, 2001.

Nixon, Joan Lowery. *Will's Story: 1771.* New York: Random House, 2001.

Samford, Patricia, and David L. Ribblett. *Archaeology for Young Explorers: Uncovering History at Colonial Williamsburg.* Williamsburg, Va.: Colonial Williamsburg Foundation, 1995.

Steen, Sandra, and Susan Steen. *Colonial Williamsburg.* New York: Dillon Press, 1993.

Wirkner, Linda. *Mystery of the Blue-Gowned Ghost.* Williamsburg, Va.: Colonial Williamsburg Foundation, 1994.

On the Web

Colonial Williamsburg Foundation

www.colonialwilliamsburg.org

For information about the foundation and its history, as well as details about visiting Colonial Williamsburg

Williamsburg Official Guide

www.williamsburg.com

For Williamsburg history and links to information about Yorktown and Jamestown, two nearby historic locations

Through the Mail

Colonial Williamsburg Foundation

P.O. Box 1776

Williamsburg, VA 23187-1776

To write for information about the foundation's work

On the Road

Colonial Williamsburg

Midway between Richmond and Norfolk on I-64

Williamsburg, VA

1-800-HISTORY

To visit the world's largest outdoor living-history museum

INDEX

American Revolution, 17, 29, 37
Association for the Preservation of
    Virginia Antiquities, 17

Botetourt, Lord, 32
Bruton Parish Church, 9, 14–15,
    15, 31

capitol, *4,* 11–12, *13,* 19, 32, 34, *34*
Civil War, 14, 30
College of William and Mary,
    8, 9, 10, *10,* 32
Colonial Williamsburg, 4–5, *5,*
    35–38, *35, 36, 37, 39,* 40, *41*
Colonial Williamsburg
    Foundation, 31, 35
construction, 11–12, 17, 19
Continental Congress, 29
Council of State, 24
craftsmen, 20, 23, *23,* 37, *37*
Currency Act, 26, 28

Duke of Gloucester Street, 10, *11,*
    14, *17*
Dunmore, John Murray, 16

French and Indian War, 28
furniture, *18,* 19–20, *20,* 32, 34, 37

gardens, 5, 12, 17, 22–23, *22,* 32–33

General Assembly, 24–25
George I, king of England, 23
George III, king of England, 26
Goodwin, W. A. R., 31
Governor's Palace, *5,* 12, 14, *14, 18,*
    19, *20, 22,* 32, 34
Gunpowder Incident, 16

Henry, Patrick, 38
House of Burgesses, 4, *4, 6,* 8, 24,
    24
houses, 17, *17,* 19–22, *21,* 32, 34,
    35, *35*

indentured servants, 7
interpreters, 37, *37,* 38, *39*

Jamestown colony, 6–7, 9, 11
Jefferson, Thomas, 10, 32, 38

kitchens, 7, 12, 21

map, *33*
Market Square, 15
Middle Plantation, 9
Monroe, James, 10

Nicholson, Francis, 9–10, 17

plantations, 7, 8, *8,* 24

powder magazine, 15–17, *16*
Publick times, 25–26, *25*

Quartering Act, 26, *27*

restoration, 5, 23, 31–35
Revenue Act, 26
Richmond, Virginia, 29–30, *30*
Rockefeller, John D., Jr., 31, *31*

slavery, 7, *8*
smokehouses, 7, 21
Stamp Act, 28–29, *28*
Sugar Act. *See* Revenue Act.

tenant farmers, 7
tobacco, 6, 7
tradesmen, 23, *23,* 37, *37*
Tyler, John, 10

Virginia colony, 4, *4,* 6, 7, 8
Virginia General Assembly, 15,
    24–25

Washington, George, 10, 38
William III, king of England,
    9, 12
Williamsburg colony, *4, 5, 10,*
    11, 13, 14, 15, 17, 21, 33, 34

About the Author

Judy Alter is the author of nearly thirty books, both fiction and nonfiction.
Her nonfiction books for young readers include *The Santa Fe Trail,*
Extraordinary Women of the American West, Rodeo: The Best Show on Dirt,
Sam Houston, Mapping the American West, and others.

　　Judy Alter is the director of a small university publishing division. She has
four children—all grown—two cats, and a large dog. Her hobbies include
cooking, reading, and gardening.